AF228849

ENGINEERING
THE EIFFEL TOWER

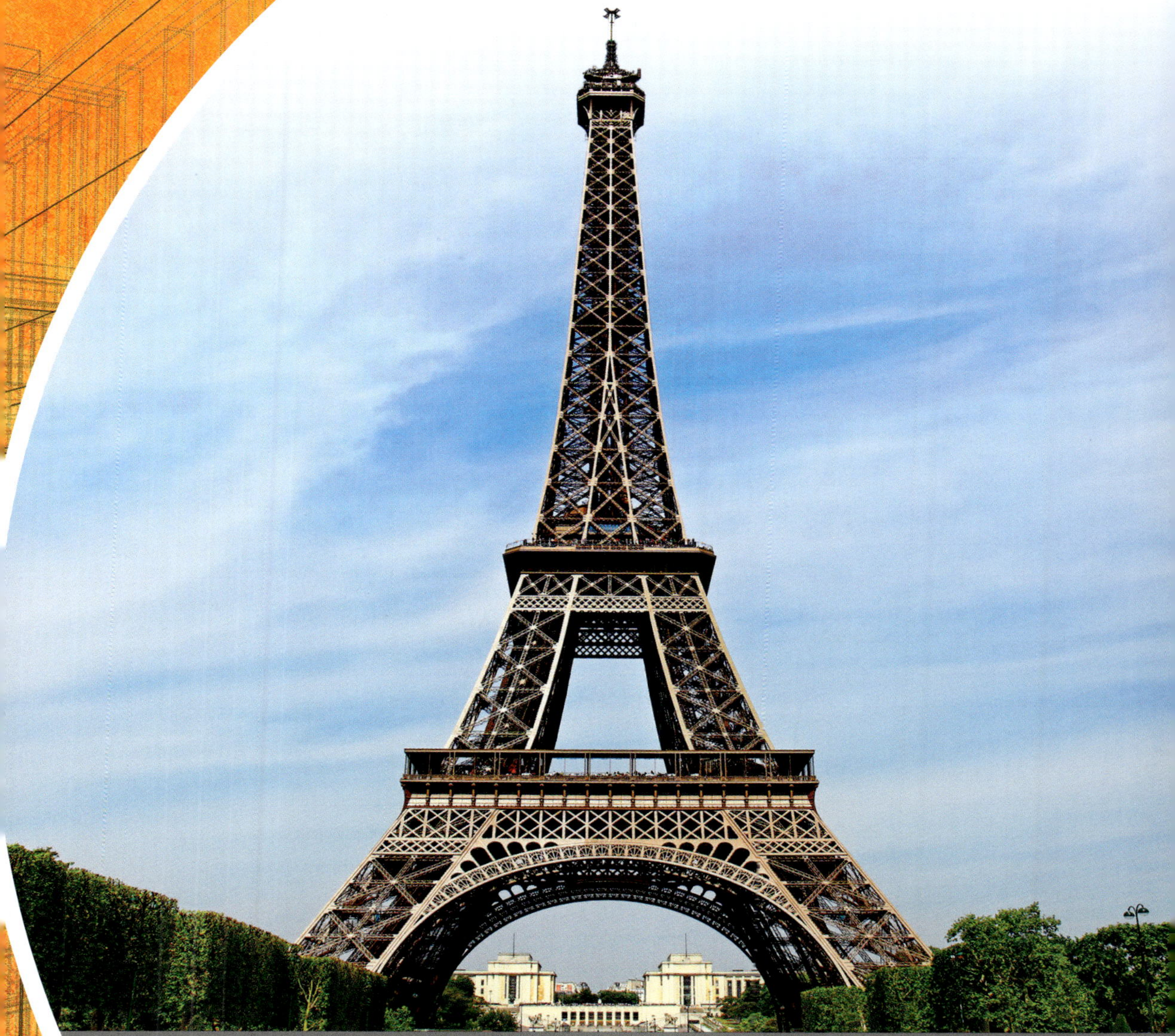

BY JANET SLINGERLAND

CONTENT CONSULTANT
Patrick Weidman
Professor Emeritus, Mechanical Engineering
University of Colorado Boulder

Cover image: The Eiffel Tower sits in the Champ de
Mars, a park in Paris, France.

Core Library

An Imprint of Abdo Publishing
abdopublishing.com

abdopublishing.com

Published by Abdo Publishing, a division of ABDO, PO Box 398166, Minneapolis, Minnesota 55439. Copyright © 2018 by Abdo Consulting Group, Inc. International copyrights reserved in all countries. No part of this book may be reproduced in any form without written permission from the publisher. Core Library™ is a trademark and logo of Abdo Publishing.

Printed in the United States of America, North Mankato, Minnesota
032017
092017

Cover Photo: Shutterstock Images
Interior Photos: Shutterstock Images, 1; Radu Razvan/Shutterstock Images, 4–5, 43; Universal History Archive/UIG/Getty Images, 7; Universal History Archive/Getty Images, 9, 19; Photo12/UIG/Getty Images, 12–13, 17 (right); Michel Gunther/Getty Images, 14–15; Maurice Koechlin, 17 (left); FPG/Hulton Archive/Getty Images, 22–23, 45; ullstein bild/Getty Images, 24; Bettmann/Getty Images, 26; ND/Roger Viollet/Getty Images, 29, 32–33; Library of Congress/Corbis/VCG/Getty Images, 30; SPL/Science Source, 35; Hulton Archive/Getty Images, 36–37; iStockphoto, 38 (left, middle left); Jozsef Bagota/Shutterstock Images, 38 (middle, middle right, right); Astrid Di Crollalanza/Gamma-Rapho/Getty Images, 39

Editor: Arnold Ringstad
Imprint Designer: Maggie Villaume
Series Design Direction: Laura Polzin

Publisher's Cataloging-in-Publication Data

Names: Slingerland, Janet, author.
Title: Engineering the Eiffel Tower / by Janet Slingerland.
Description: Minneapolis, MN : Abdo Publishing, 2018. | Series: Building by design | Includes bibliographical references and index.
Identifiers: LCCN 2017930240 | ISBN 9781532111655 (lib. bdg.) | ISBN 9781680789508 (ebook)
Subjects: LCSH: Structural engineering--Miscellanea--Juvenile literature. | Eiffel Tower (Paris, France)--Design and construction--Juvenile literature. | Civil engineering--Juvenile literature. | Buildings, structures, etc.--Juvenile literature. | Buildings--Miscellanea--Juvenile literature.
Classification: DDC 624--dc23
LC record available at http://lccn.loc.gov/2017930240

CONTENTS

CHAPTER
ONE

THE IRON LADY

Streams of tourists exit a line of buses. They all look up to the sky, whipping out their cell phones and cameras. Every few feet, groups are huddled together. They are having their pictures taken. They are all here to see one of the most famous structures in the world: the Eiffel Tower.

The Eiffel Tower was built as part of a World's Fair in Paris, France, in 1889. Originally, the plan was to take the tower down after 20 years. More than 125 years later, the Eiffel Tower is more popular than ever. It has earned the nickname *"la dame de fer,"* or *"the*

Each year, millions of people visit the Eiffel Tower and the surrounding park.

PERSPECTIVES
CELEBRATION CONTROVERSY

Turning the 1889 Exposition into an anniversary party for the French Revolution created some controversy. Many countries refused to participate. The United Kingdom, Italy, and Russia still had ruling monarchs. They would not acknowledge an event that celebrated a revolution. Ultimately, representatives from 43 nations attended the fair. Sixteen of them went without the approval of their governments.

iron lady." This iron tower has become a symbol of Paris.

MAKING A STATEMENT

World's Fairs have been happening since the mid-1800s. Every few years, a country hosts one of these events. Nations set up exhibits to share their cultures and technology.

Paris hosted a World's Fair in 1889 known as the Exposition Universelle. Organizers used the event as a celebration of the one-hundredth anniversary of the French Revolution. They hoped to show modern France

The Exposition Universelle featured a vast exhibit hall with displays from various nations.

to the world. To do this, they believed the fair needed something special. It needed a structure to represent French culture. The planners wanted something bold. They decided on a tower 984 feet (300 m) tall. The structure would dwarf all others in the world.

The organizers held a competition to design the tower. People submitted more than 100 entries. Some were elegant. Others were absurd. One entry proposed a giant watering can. Another suggested an enormous guillotine.

The two main competitors were engineer Gustave Eiffel and architect Jules Bourdais. Eiffel proposed an iron tower. Bourdais presented a classical stone structure. It would be topped by an electrical beacon. The beacon would light the night for miles around.

Eiffel argued that existing cathedrals had already reached the maximum height for stone structures. Bourdais mocked Eiffel's iron design. He claimed his tower would cost far less than Eiffel's. The Bourdais plan had the tower resting on the ground. Eiffel knew such a tower needed an underground foundation. The committee finally decided the tower had to be a metal structure. Only Eiffel's tower met this requirement.

FACING OPPOSITION

Winning the competition was just the beginning for Eiffel. He still needed to find funding. He also had to

Eiffel's legacy has lived on in the name of his famous tower.

A WARY PUBLIC

Many Parisians feared the proposed tower would collapse. They had good reasons for their concern. Less than ten years earlier, an engineering failure cost the lives of 75 people in the United Kingdom. On December 28, 1879, strong winds caused the collapse of the Tay Bridge. A train plummeted from the iron bridge into the sea below.

overcome serious opposition. Local residents worried the tower would collapse on their homes. Eiffel publicly claimed full responsibility for any damage caused by his tower.

Other Parisians still had concerns. More than 300 prominent citizens formed a committee. Their goal was to stop the building of the tower. In February 1887, they issued a written protest. Eiffel defended his tower. In the end, the tower was built. The controversy continued for decades. But today the Eiffel Tower is celebrated as France's most famous landmark.

STRAIGHT TO THE
SOURCE

On February 14, 1887, a letter appeared in the French newspaper *Le Temps*. In it, a group of citizens detailed their opposition to the Eiffel Tower:

> *We come, writers, painters, sculptors, architects, passionate lovers of the beauty of Paris—a beauty until now unspoiled—to protest with all our might, with all our outrage, in the name of slighted French taste, in the name of threatened French art and history, against the erection, in the heart of our capital, of the useless and monstrous Eiffel Tower.*
>
> *Are we going to allow all this beauty and tradition to be profaned? Is Paris now to be associated with the grotesque and mercantile imagination of a machine builder, to be defaced and disgraced?*
>
> Source: Arthur Chandler. "Revolution: The Paris Exposition Universelle, 1889." *Arthur Chandler's New Home Page*. Arthur Chandler, n.d. Web. Accessed October 10, 2016.

Consider Your Audience

This passage was written more 125 years ago. Imagine the Eiffel Tower were being proposed today. How would people today write a letter in opposition to such a tower? Write a blog post conveying this same information for a modern audience.

CHAPTER
TWO

A MAN WITH A PLAN

When built in the 1880s, the planned Eiffel Tower would be almost twice the height of the tallest structure at that time. Building such a massive tower required lots of planning and specialized knowledge.

Eiffel studied many different subjects in school. He learned engineering, history, and literature. His main area of study was chemistry. Eiffel graduated in 1855. He began a career in metallurgy. Most of his early work involved railway bridges. He soon had his own business.

In the mid-1800s, before the tower's construction, the only way to get a bird's-eye view of Paris was from a balloon.

In 1877 his company completed the world's longest

iron arch bridge. The Ponte Maria Bridge spanned

525 feet (160 m) across the Douro River in Portugal.

Eiffel built the bridge from both sides of the river.

This technique reduced costs and limited the need for

scaffolding. Each bank held support piers. The sections of the bridge were held in place by cables attached to these piers until they connected.

In 1884 Eiffel completed the Garabit Viaduct in France. The bridge spanned a very windy section of the

SUPPORTING LADY LIBERTY

In 1879, Gustave Eiffel was given an unexpected career opportunity. On September 17, architect Eugene Viollet-le-Duc died. He left his work on the Statue of Liberty's inner structure unfinished. Sculptor Auguste Bartholdi asked Eiffel to step in and finish the project. Viollet-le-Duc's design had used sand-filled stone compartments to hold up the statue's copper exterior. Eiffel replaced that with a flexible metal skeleton.

Truyère River. Eiffel's design was wider at the bases and narrower at the top. This reduced the amount of the bridge that came into contact with the wind. He did not use traditional solid beams. Eiffel used trusses made up of many metal triangles. With less material for the wind to hit, the bridge would be more stable.

DESIGNED FOR WIND RESISTANCE

The design of the tower began in 1884. Like the Garabit Viaduct, the tower would be wide at the bottom and narrow at the top. It would be made out of triangular metal pieces. This would reduce the effect of wind.

COMBINING ENGINEERING AND ARCHITECTURE

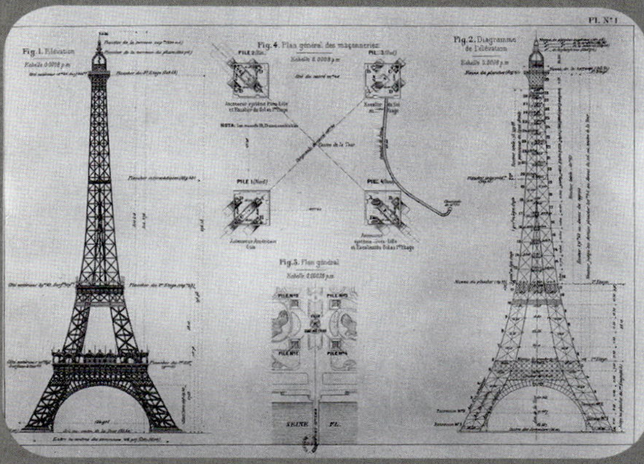

Two of Eiffel's engineers, Emile Nouguier and Maurice Koechlin, created the tower's initial design on the left. The final design is on the right. Compare the two designs. How are they different? How are they the same? Which design do you like better? Why?

The tower design called for a base with four pillars. They would rise up to meet at a platform 187 feet (57 m) above the ground. Two more floors would be placed at 377 feet (115 m) and 906 feet (276 m). The piers were tilted inward as they rose. This provided maximum wind resistance. It also made the tower more stable.

A team of 50 engineers and designers worked on the tower's plans for three years. They created 5,300 drawings detailing how the tower would be built. The tower needed to be easy to dismantle. The contract stated it would be taken down after 20 years. The plans called for the tower's 18,038 iron parts to be made in Eiffel's factory outside Paris. At the construction site, the pieces would be put together.

MAKING THE IRON

Today, steel is the most common building material for tall structures. But the Eiffel Tower was built before steel was a standard part of construction. Instead, it was built using puddled iron.

The iron came from mines outside Paris. Mined iron ore contains elements such as silicon and sulfur. Before the iron could be used, these impurities needed to be removed. This was done by heating the iron ore.

To create the Eiffel Tower's iron, ironmakers first put layers of charcoal, flux, and iron ore in a blast furnace.

Metallurgists had been making forms of iron for hundreds of years prior to the tower's construction.

As the iron melted, it would absorb carbon from the charcoal. The molten metal would run off into molds. The result was pig iron. Pig iron is a type of cast iron. Cast iron contains between 3 and 4.5 percent carbon. This high carbon content makes cast iron hard and brittle. Heavy blows can crack or shatter it.

Ironmakers then took pig iron and put it through a puddling process. The pig iron was heated in a puddling furnace. When the iron melted, some of the carbon burned off. The removal of the carbon increased the iron's melting point. This caused semi-solid bits of iron to form in the molten metal. A worker called a puddler continually stirred the metal. This removed the semi-solid bits. Hammering or rolling removed the remaining impurities. The iron was finally ready for use in the enormous structure.

STRAIGHT TO THE
SOURCE

Gustave Eiffel wrote a response to the opponents of his tower:

Do people think that because we are engineers, beauty plays no part in what we build, that if we aim for the solid and lasting, that we don't at the same time do our utmost to achieve elegance? . . . I maintain that the curves . . . of the monument . . . will give a great impression of strength and beauty. . . . [T]here's an attraction in things colossal, a special charm to which theories of ordinary art are hardly applicable. Will we maintain that it's because of their artistic value that the Pyramids have so fired the imagination of men? After all, are they anything other than artificial hillocks? Yet what visitor remains unmoved in their presence? Who has not returned from them filled with an admiration that is irresistible? And what is the source of this admiration, if not the immensity of effort and the grandeur of the result?

Source: "All You Need to Know About the Eiffel Tower."
La Tour Eiffel. The Eiffel Tower Operating Company, n.d.
Web. Accessed October 10, 2016.

What's the Big Idea?

Take a close look at Eiffel's response. What is the main point he is making? Pick out two or three pieces of evidence he uses to make his point.

THE IRON MAGICIAN

Workers broke ground for the tower's foundation on January 28, 1887. More than 100 workers labored in Eiffel's factory, creating the tower's iron parts. Another group of 150 to 300 workers assembled the pieces at the building site. Eiffel's careful planning resulted in a speedy construction process. The enormous tower was finished in just two years, two months, and five days. This feat earned Eiffel the nickname "*le magicien du fer*," or "the iron magician."

Workers began piecing together the massive tower in 1887.

Building a stout, sturdy foundation would be key to the tower's success.

SOLID FOUNDATIONS

When construction began, the workers didn't start building upward. Instead, they dug down. Each of the tower's four piers needed a foundation. A building's foundation is like the roots of a tree. It helps keep the structure anchored to the ground.

The foundations needed to be set deep underground. Two of the slabs were about 23 feet (7 m) down. The piers set near the river were more difficult. Those foundations needed to start 40 feet (12 m) below the ground. This was below the water level of the river.

Workers pushed watertight metal caissons below the water. These caissons were like giant metal boxes. The bottom of each caisson was open. Workers descended into the caissons. They dug out the dirt below the caissons until they hit the gravel bed.

When the caissons reached the water line, workers pumped air into them. The compressed air kept water out. It allowed the workers to continue to dig until they reached the desired depth. The caissons were then filled with concrete. This formed the base of the foundations.

WITH CAREFUL PRECISION

The foundations were in place by July 1887. Finally, the workers could start building upward. This stage of the tower's construction was the most critical. The four piers

Once construction reached the first platform, Eiffel ensured the rest of the tower would be even and stable.

were built independently. But they had to meet at just the right heights and angles. The first platform had to be perfectly horizontal. If it were uneven, it wouldn't be safe to build the rest of the tower.

Eiffel ensured the first platform could be leveled to within one millimeter of true horizontal. The legs of the tower were built on hydraulic jacks and sand boxes. If a column were too high, sand could be let out to bring it down to the right height. If it were too low, the hydraulic jack would be used to bring it up a bit.

Wooden scaffolding supported the piers as they grew. Since they were angled, the piers would not be stable until they reached the first platform. Once the piers were all connected, the tower was sturdy.

RIVETING WORK

The tower's pieces were connected using metal rivets. It took 2.5 million rivets to put the tower together. Most of them were put in place in the factory. Only one-third were installed at the construction site.

Once a metal part was placed, rivets were added to secure it.

It took a team of four to place the rivets. One man heated the rivet. A second held a heated rivet in its proper place. A third shaped the heads on both sides of the beam. The fourth flattened the rivet with a hammer.

GOING UP

As the tower got taller, lifting parts into place became more difficult. Eiffel came up with a plan to make this easier. He used the elevators that would later carry visitors up the tower.

Elevators rode along tracks in the four legs of the tower. To carry iron components to the top, Eiffel used cranes that hooked into these tracks. These cranes

The tower's elevators proved useful both during construction and after the tower was finished.

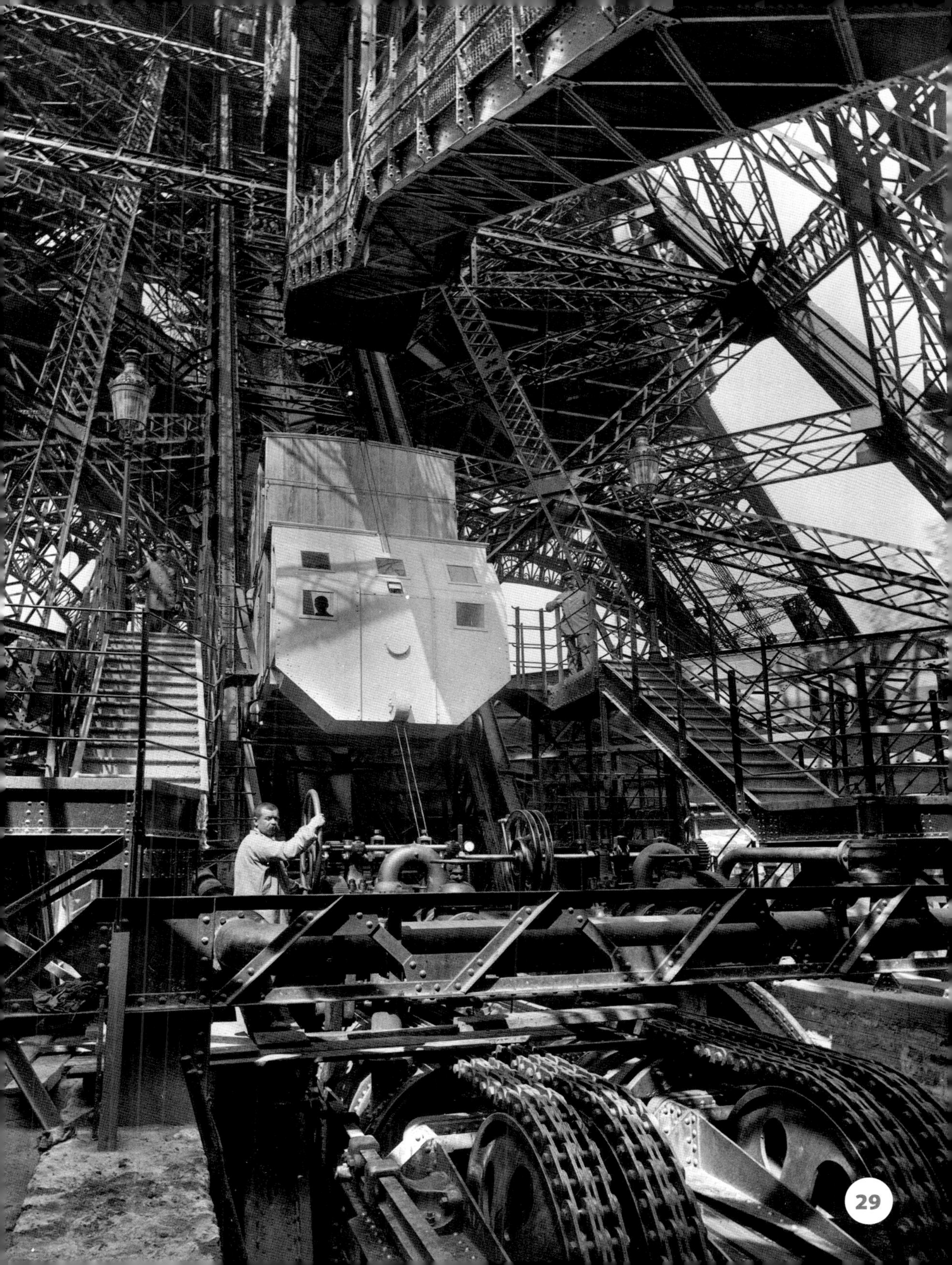

moved as the lift tracks were installed. They steadily
rose up the tower. Workers installed additional cranes
on the platforms.

The Eiffel Tower was completed in 1889. It opened
to the public on May 15. Nearly two million people
visited the tower. They looked out over Paris from
incredible heights. At night, the iron tower was lit by
hundreds of lamps. Beams of light in the colors of the

French flag—blue, white, and red—shone over the city from the top of the tower.

Visitors accessed the first two platforms by the elevators on the tower's legs. These elevators had one or two cabins in which people sat. They were a cross between a lift and a cable car. They wouldn't look out of place in a modern amusement park.

To ascend to the third platform, visitors had to use a pair of elevators that ran up the center of the tower. Only one elevator ascended at a time. At the same time, another elevator descended. The two elevators counter-balanced one another.

EXPLORE ONLINE

One crucial component of the Eiffel Tower covered in Chapter Three is its elevator system. Explore the website below to find out more about the past and present elevators in the tower. What did you learn from the website?

THE EIFFEL TOWER'S LIFTS

abdocorelibrary.com/engineering-the-eiffel-tower

SAVING THE TOWER

Eiffel knew his tower was slated to be taken down after just 20 years. He believed he could extend its life if it proved useful to science. The day after it opened, Eiffel opened a laboratory on the tower. He installed equipment to measure the weather. Barometers measured air pressure. Wind gauges measured the wind.

Before long, Eiffel began to conduct aerodynamics experiments. He attached a cable from the tower's second floor to the ground. He dropped various objects down the cable. Then he observed the how the objects

The completed tower became the centerpiece of the 1889 World's Fair.

A MONUMENT TO SCIENCE

From the beginning, Eiffel made his tower a monument to science. He had the names of 72 scientists engraved on the side of the tower. The honorees include mathematicians, chemists, engineers, and more. Over the years, the names disappeared under layers of paint. An effort in the 1980s restored this tribute to science. The list of names can also be found on the official Eiffel Tower website.

interacted with the air as they fell.

In the early 1900s, he built a wind tunnel at the base of the tower. He carried out more than 5,000 tests in the wind tunnel. He documented his findings in several books. The most popular of these, *The Resistance of Air and Aviation*, came out in 1913.

RADIO DAYS

Around the time the Eiffel Tower was being built, an invention was being developed that would help save it. Until that time, long-distance communication was

difficult. Letters sent through the mail could take weeks to arrive. Telegraph messages could be sent almost instantly. However, they could be sent only over wires between fixed points. Wireless broadcasting technology would forever change the way the world communicated.

Radio waves transmitted through the air did not rely on wires. Any receiver within range of the signal could receive it. Telegraph messages could be sent this way. So could radio and television transmissions.

The height of the Eiffel Tower made it a prime spot for a transmission station. The first wireless telegraph message was sent from the tower in 1898. In 1899, wireless signals were sent from the tower across the English Channel to England. By 1909, the Eiffel Tower had proved useful for military communication. In 1910,

the City of Paris renewed Eiffel's permit for another
70 years.

JUST KEEP PAINTING

The Eiffel Tower requires constant maintenance. One of
the biggest jobs is painting. This is needed to protect

REACHING TO THE SKY

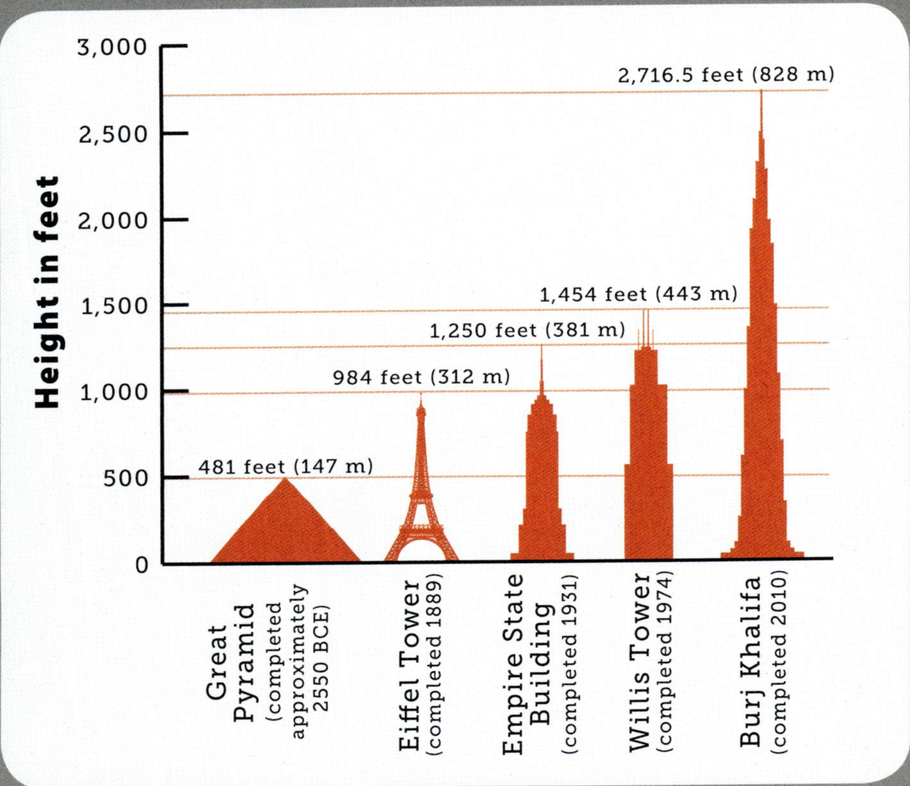

The Eiffel Tower was the tallest structure in the world for more than 40 years. Take a look at a few structures that were the tallest in the world at the time of their construction. How does this graph help you understand the significance of the Eiffel Tower?

the iron structure. If left unprotected, the tower's iron would rust, making the tower unsafe.

The whole tower needs to be painted every seven years. This process takes 25 painters 18 months to

complete. The methods used by painters today are the
same as those used during Eiffel's time. All work is done
by hand.

Prior to starting, safety nets are hung below the
work area. Painters wear harnesses connected to safety

RETURN OF THE MAGIC

In 2014 the Eiffel Tower celebrated its 125th anniversary with a new addition. A portion of the first platform was replaced with a transparent floor. Visitors can stand on the floor and view the ground 187 feet (57 m) below. It has become a popular spot for smartphone selfies. Anne Hidalgo, mayor of Paris at the time, praised the change. She felt it would bring some magic back to the city while staying true to its history.

lines that attach to the tower. All tools are attached to the painters' belts or wrists. This prevents the tools from falling on pedestrians below the tower.

The work starts on the most corroded parts of the tower. Any rust is stripped off and an antirust primer is applied. A second antirust primer coat provides added protection against the elements. The final coat of paint is decorative.

Since 1968 the Eiffel Tower has been painted the same color. It is officially known as Eiffel Tower Brown.

Three shades of the color are used. The darkest covers the lowest portion of the tower. The lightest is at the top.

Maintenance and painting have kept the Eiffel Tower standing for more than 125 years. Visitors can still feel the thrill of looking down upon Paris from high atop the structure. Gustave Eiffel's vision has become a permanent symbol of the city.

FURTHER EVIDENCE

Chapter Four discusses how the Eiffel Tower survived beyond its initial expiration date. What is one of the main points of this chapter? What evidence is included to support this point? Read the article at the website below. Does it support the main point of the chapter? What new information does it provide?

HOW SCIENCE SAVED THE EIFFEL TOWER
abdocorelibrary.com/engineering-the-eiffel-tower

FAST FACTS

- The Eiffel Tower was built in Paris, France, as part of the Exposition Universelle, a World's Fair held in 1889.

- Engineer Gustave Eiffel designed the tower.

- Eiffel had a background in metallurgy and construction before building the tower.

- The tower's design called for a base with four pillars, connected with platforms and meeting as they near the top of the tower.

- The Eiffel Tower was constructed with puddled iron.

- The first step in construction was digging down to create foundations for the pillars.

- Eiffel devised a method of keeping the four pillars at even heights as workers prepared to build the first connecting platform.

- The tower's elevator tracks were used during construction to help lift components to the top of the tower.

- The tower was planned to stand for only 20 years, but its usefulness for scientific experiments and radio broadcasts led to it being left in place.

- Extensive painting is needed on a regular basis to prevent the iron tower from rusting.

STOP AND
THINK

Tell the Tale

Chapter Four discusses the job of painting the Eiffel Tower. Imagine you are a painter working on the tower. Write 200 words about your job painting the tower. In what time period are you working? What concerns do you have as you do your job? How important do you think your job is?

Surprise Me

After reading this book, what two or three facts about the Eiffel Tower did you find most surprising? Write a few sentences about each fact. Why did you find them surprising?

Dig Deeper

After reading this book, what questions do you still have about the Eiffel Tower? With an adult's help, find some reliable sources that can help answer your questions. Write a paragraph about what you learned.

Say What?

Engineers and scientists tend to use lots of complicated words. Find five words in this book you are unfamiliar with. Use a dictionary to find out what they mean. Then write the meanings in your own words and use each word in a new sentence.

GLOSSARY

aerodynamics
a branch of science that deals with the forces exerted by air or other gases in motion

caisson
a watertight chamber used in building foundations and in underwater construction

dismantle
to take apart

flux
a substance added to a furnace during metalworking to help remove impurities

guillotine
an execution device used to cut people's heads off

horizontal
parallel to the ground; flat and level

metallurgy
the science of extracting metals from ore, refining metals, and mixing metals together to obtain alloys with desired properties

rivet
a metal bolt with a head at one end; the plain end is flattened after passing through the parts it holds together

scaffolding
an elevated platform that allows workers access to out-of-reach areas of a construction project

LEARN MORE

Books

Cornille, Didier. *Who Built That? Skyscrapers: An Introduction to Skyscrapers and Their Architects.* New York: Princeton Architectural, 2014.

Roberts, Russell. *Eiffel Tower.* Kennett Square, PA: Purple Toad Publishing, 2016.

Roeder, Annette, and Jane Michael. *13 Buildings Children Should Know.* New York: Prestel, 2009.

Websites

To learn more about Building by Design, visit **abdobooklinks.com**. These links are routinely monitored and updated to provide the most current information available.

Visit **abdocorelibrary.com** for free additional tools for teachers and students.

INDEX

About the Author

Before writing books, Janet Slingerland was an engineer, using computers to work on things such as telephones and airplanes. Janet lives in New Jersey with her husband and three children.